# How to Reap
# 100-Fold
## in a Year of Famine

Andrew Wommack

© Copyright 2025 – Andrew Wommack

Printed in the United States of America. All rights reserved. No portion of this book may be reproduced, stored in a retrieval system, or transmitted in any form or by any means—electronic, mechanical, photocopy, recording, scanning, or other—except for brief quotations in critical reviews or articles, without the prior written permission of the publisher.

Unless otherwise indicated, all Scripture quotations are taken from the King James Version® of the Bible. Copyright © by the British Crown. Public domain.

Published by Andrew Wommack Ministries, Inc.

Woodland Park, CO 80863

ISBN 13 TP: 978-1-59548-785-8

For Worldwide Distribution, Printed in the USA

1 2 3 4 5 6 / 28 27 26 25

# Contents

Introduction .................................................................. 1

"It Came to Pass" ......................................................... 2

It All Depends On Your Perspective ........................... 14

Your Situation Isn't Unique ......................................... 17

Get a Specific Word from God .................................... 24

What Is God's Word to You? ........................................ 25

Conclusion .................................................................. 47

Receive Jesus as Your Savior ..................................... 51

Receive the Holy Spirit ............................................... 53

Would you like to get more out of this teaching?

Scan the QR code to access this teaching in video or audio formats to help you dive even deeper as you study.

Accessing the teaching this way will help you get even more out of this booklet.

**awmi.net/browse**

# Introduction

We don't have to learn everything through the "school of hard knocks." There is a better way.

First Corinthians 10:6-11 says that everything recorded in the Old Testament was written for our example so that we could learn through others what to do and what not to do. With that in mind, I want to share some great truths from Genesis 26 about Isaac, who sowed in a year of famine and reaped a one-hundred-fold return in that same year.

The dictionary defines "famine" as "extreme scarcity of food."[1] The actual Hebrew word used in Genesis 26:1 simply means "hunger."[2] But it can apply to other extremes besides just scarcity of or hunger for food. Amos 8:11 speaks of a famine of hearing the words of the Lord.

*Behold, the days come, saith the Lord God, that I will send a famine in the land, not a famine of bread, nor a thirst for water, but of hearing the words of the* LORD:

So, a lack of hearing the true word of God was called a famine. There can also be a famine of finances. That's what I want to address in this booklet. Maybe you are in a financial famine now. If so, I've got good news for you. Just as Isaac reaped one-hundred-fold in a year of famine, you can too.

## "It Came to Pass"

Prosperity ebbs and flows in all societies. There are times of boom and bust, but it is a fact that hard times are opportunities for those who don't panic. Most millionaires are made during hard times. They look past the immediate crisis, take advantage of the situation, buy assets for pennies on the dollar, and then sell for huge profits when the economy turns around. Likewise, hard times or famines are opportunities for those who trust God.

That's what happened with Isaac.

*Then Isaac sowed in that land, and received in the same year an hundredfold: and the LORD blessed him.*

Genesis 26:12

To reap a hundredfold at any time is exceptional, but to do that in a time of famine is very rare and something that should make us all stand up and take notice. There are lessons from Isaac's experience that should inspire and equip us all to follow his example. God is no respecter of persons (Rom. 2:11). What He did for Isaac, He can and will do for any of us if we believe Him.

The first thing I want to point out is in Genesis 26:1, which says,

*And there was a famine in the land, beside the first famine that was in the days of Abraham...*

God doesn't waste words or put things in Scripture as fillers. There is a purpose for stating this wasn't the first famine in the land. That's an important point.

One of the lessons to learn from this is that famines come and go. This wasn't the first famine, and it wouldn't be the last. Unless we put things into their proper perspective, the devil will blow our current famine all out of proportion and make us think our situation is unique. It's not. We must keep that in mind in hard times.

One of my favorite scriptures is, "It came to pass." I like to say it this way: "That's why it came; it was so it could pass." We have to put our hardships into their proper perspective. Hard times never last, but those who put their trust in the Lord do.

> *They that trust in the* Lord *shall be as mount Zion, which cannot be removed, but abideth for ever.*
>
> Psalm 125:1

The Lord's plans for us are always good.

> *For I know the plans I have for you," declares the* Lord, *"plans to prosper you and not to harm you, plans to give you hope and a future.*

Jeremiah 29:11, *New International Version*

He delights in the prosperity of His servants.

*Let them shout for joy, and be glad, that favour my righteous cause: yea, let them say continually, Let the* Lord *be magnified, which hath pleasure in the prosperity of his servant.*

Psalm 35:27

The Lord is pleased when we prosper, and conversely, He's not pleased when we don't prosper. His will is for us to prosper and be healthy, just as much as He wants us to prosper in our souls.

*Beloved, I wish above all things that thou mayest prosper and be in health, even as thy soul prospereth.*

3 John 1:2

Since it is the Lord's will for us to prosper, any financial hardship is outside of God's will. This is something I've learned over fifty-seven years of walking with the Lord. I've been in financial straits numerous times, and the Lord has brought me through them all.

We have not only survived, but we've thrived. Patience is the ability to stay in faith over a prolonged period of time, and having experienced God's supernatural provision on many occasions has exercised my patience (James 1:3). The Lord has been faithful to me, and I know He's faithful to you too.

That's the attitude the Apostle Paul took towards all his sufferings.

> *For our light affliction, which is but for a moment, worketh for us a far more exceeding and eternal weight of glory; While we look not at the things which are seen, but at the things which are not seen: for the things which are seen are temporal; but the things which are not seen are eternal.*
>
> 2 Corinthians 4:17-18

The word "temporal" in verse 18 means "temporary."[3] That's a key. Everything that we can see, taste, hear, smell, or feel (our five senses) is temporary. But the truths regarding our financial success are eternal truths revealed in God's Word, which should give us hope. We must keep our eyes on the promises, not the problems.

When Jamie and I first married, I decided to quit my job and go full time in ministry. My heart was right, but my head was wrong. I learned later that a minister's support is proportional to his ministry (1 Cor. 9:14). I was only ministering to a few people in a small Bible study, so I should have kept working until the numbers increased. Because of my wrong thinking, Jamie and I were extremely poor.

Our first tax return as a couple only showed $1,253 income for twelve months, and we had a rent payment of $100 per month. I really don't know how we survived. Praise God for Jamie, who never once complained to me. I suspect she had some serious conversations with the Lord about my not working, but she never said anything to me. She has always been supportive, even when I've made it hard on her. Praise God for a godly wife.

Just a few months into this "living by faith," we were in dire straits. We went for days without any food and were down to our last seventy-five cents. We didn't have credit cards back then or a checking account. We were stone broke.

Jamie took our last three quarters and drove our car to a laundromat to wash some clothes. While she was gone, I got into some serious prayer with the Lord. I was telling him that He had to do something about our lack of food. Actually, I was complaining, not praying. I told Him I would give my right arm to feed Jamie. At that exact moment, He spoke to me through Luke 12:32, which says,

> *Fear not, little flock; for it is your Father's good pleasure to give you the kingdom.*

He lovingly rebuked me for thinking that I loved Jamie more than He did. He not only wanted to meet our needs but had already done it (Eph. 1:3). I just needed to believe.

I had taken my eyes off God's Word and was looking at our problem, and just like Peter when he took his eyes off Jesus, I was beginning to sink (Matt. 14:30). I had begun to doubt God's love for us, and fear and doubt were knocking at my door. That scripture pointed me back to God's love and assured me that He wanted us to prosper more than I wanted us to prosper. He told me, "I gave my Son to prosper you."

> *For ye know the grace of our Lord Jesus Christ, that, though he was rich, yet for your sakes he became poor, that ye through his poverty might be rich.*
>
> 2 Corinthians 8:9

I fell to my knees and repented of doubting God's love for us and started praising Him that we were going to see His provision that day. When Jamie got back from washing our clothes, I told her what the Lord had spoken to me and assured her that we were going to have a meal that day. At lunch, we had nothing. At supper, we had nothing, but our faith was strong that we would eat before midnight.

We went to church that evening, and afterward, a friend invited us over to their apartment. We didn't say anything to them about our situation, but we were hopeful that they would offer us something to eat. We visited with them for nearly an hour, but there wasn't even an offer of something to drink. Eventually, we got up to leave and head home.

Before we left, our friend said, "There is something I want to give you. I came over to your apartment this morning, but your car was gone, so I thought I would just wait until this evening to give it to you." Then he brought out about ten or twenty pounds of fish and all the trimmings to go with them.

The only time our car was gone from our apartment that day was the time that Jamie took it to wash clothes, and I was in the apartment receiving this revelation from the Lord. At that exact moment, this friend came with God's supply, but it would be about twelve hours before we actually got to eat it.

We rushed home, Jamie cooked it up, and we ate a meal just a few minutes before midnight. The next day was my birthday, and a lady in our church gave us a whole cardboard box of porterhouse steaks. We went from famine to feast, all because I got my eyes back on the Lord and rejected all unbelief about Him providing for us. The provision existed the moment I believed, but it took a while before we could see it.

Likewise, God has already commanded a blessing upon you in everything you set your hand to. The Lord's blessings are chasing after you. You are blessed coming in and going out. You are above only and not beneath (Deut. 28:1-14). You are already blessed (Eph. 1:3). God's provision exists before your need.

Remembering that miraculous provision of the Lord for us way back in 1973, and all the hundreds of times I've seen Him come through for us since then, has given me a confidence that what He's done in the past, He will do again. So, the financial challenges I face today are not the first time I've been in need, and it probably won't be the last. The fact that I've survived famines in the past gives me hope for the present and the future.

I once hired a former banker to be the manager of my ministry. He was used to having a steady income in his bank. If the people who had borrowed money didn't pay, he would turn them over to a collection agency. However, the ministry doesn't work that way. Even those who have committed to being partners with us don't always follow through on their pledges. My income fluctuates every month. He was shocked.

The first month he worked for me, he told me our expenses were more than our income. I acknowledged that and thanked him for letting me know. Then the next month, the same thing happened. He was beginning to panic, and he explained to me that this was the second month in a row we were in the red. Then this happened again, and for the third month in a row, our income was down. This time, he pushed the panic button and told me I wasn't paying attention. We had to do something, and quickly.

But I had a different take on the situation. It wasn't the first time we had been in a situation like that. There was a time at the beginning of our ministry when we were nearly $60,000 behind, which was about six months' worth of income at the time. I was holding our annual board meeting, and they told me we were bankrupt. We were going to have to shut down the ministry. I didn't believe that was going to happen, but on paper, they were correct. I couldn't argue with the facts. I didn't know what to do, so I asked them to just pray with me about it.

While we were praying, my mother called. She was the one who opened our mail, and she had just received a $60,000 check in the mail. It came from a church where I had never ministered before, and to this day, I haven't ever been to that church. It was the biggest blessing we had ever received at that time. It was exactly the amount we needed to pay our bills.

That experience gave me a different perspective for the next time we faced a similar situation. In fact, it allowed me to see things differently from this manager. I shared that testimony with him and told him to wait and see what the Lord would do. Sure enough, the Lord provided, and we made it through that famine too.

This is the first step in seeing God's supernatural supply in your life. You must know that He loves you and wants you to prosper. Faith works by love (Gal. 5:6). If your total confidence in God's love for you falters, your faith will waver, and you won't receive anything from the Lord.

> But let him ask in faith, nothing wavering. For he that wavereth is like a wave of the sea driven with the wind and tossed. For let not that man think that he shall receive any thing of the Lord.
> James 1:6-7

## It All Depends On Your Perspective

Paul suffered more than most, yet he described all his troubles as just a *"light affliction,"* not because he didn't have problems but because of the way he viewed them. He said they were *"but for a moment."* The next verse revealed he wasn't looking at things in the natural world, but he was looking at things from an eternal perspective.

> For our light affliction, which is but for a moment, worketh for us a far more exceeding and eternal weight of glory; While we look not at the things which are seen, but at the things which are not seen: for the things which are

*seen* are *temporal; but the things which are not seen* are *eternal.*

2 Corinthians 4:17-18

Remembering that your situation isn't the first nor the last famine people have ever experienced will help you put everything in perspective and be encouraged to persevere through it.

As 1 Corinthians 10:13 says,

*There hath no temptation taken you but such as is common to man: but God is faithful, who will not suffer you to be tempted above that ye are able; but will with the temptation also make a way to escape, that ye may be able to bear* it.

In our fallen world, we are going to have problems, or you could say famines. That is what this verse says is common among men. We shouldn't think it strange that financial challenges come. God is not the one who created the monetary system. He doesn't have money in heaven. The monetary system is a human invention with all the flaws of other human endeavors. The Lord gives us the power to get wealth (Deut. 8:18).

He doesn't give us money directly. He will bless what we set our hand unto (Deut. 28:8), and cause men to give money into our bosom (Luke 6:38). But the Lord doesn't directly control people and their money.

I learned this back in the 1980s. Two prominent media ministers' sins were publicly exposed, and one of them went to jail. People's confidence in media ministers plummeted. Our income went down by forty percent. I didn't do anything wrong, yet we were lumped in with what others did, and it affected our finances. I've also experienced that every time there is a national crisis that grabs people's attention, they stay glued to the news and quit watching our program. That affects our income. Those things are completely beyond my control. It's not due to something I've done.

Just as Isaac found himself in a famine that was not of his making, we all have to deal with financial fluctuations beyond our control. Whether you are dependent on gifts as I am, self-employed, or work for someone else, there will be times of famine that you have to deal with. This world monetary system always goes through periods of feast and famine. We don't need to think it strange when this happens.

Satan loves to discourage us, and nothing will do that quicker than thinking that our situation is unique and, therefore, beyond hope. Regardless of what kind of famine we find ourselves in, others have gone through the same things before us and survived and even thrived. We can too. If the enemy can get us to think that our situation is unique, then we will discount what has worked for others. But the truth is that what worked for Isaac will work for us today.

I'm not minimizing the situation you are in. We all face giants from time to time, but we have to remember that we have giant-killing faith. No one would have cheered for David if he had killed a dwarf. They would have arrested him. So, the bigger the challenge, the greater the victory.

## Your Situation Isn't Unique

Another truth we must recognize is that just as this is not the first famine, it certainly won't be the last. It's prudent to recognize that, regardless of how prosperous things are in the present, there will be adversity in the future. We live in a fallen world, and one thing we can count on is problems. Jesus said,

> ...In the world ye shall have tribulation: but be of good cheer; I have overcome the world.
>
> John 16:33

Bad things happen to good people. The famine that Isaac found himself in wasn't of his own making. He didn't cause the drought, yet it affected him.

If you find yourself in a drought of your own making, you need to repent and get back on track with what God has planned for your life. There is plenty of forgiveness and grace to help you overcome anything that comes at you, even if it's your fault. God hasn't forsaken you. He's still with you (Heb. 13:5).

You can see this very clearly in Genesis 26. Isaac lied and told people Rebekah was his sister, not his wife (Gen. 26:7). He did this out of fear that someone would kill him to gain access to Rebekah because she was so beautiful. There's no way to whitewash this. That's wrong! Yet the Lord protected Isaac and Rebekah, and they prospered anyway.

If your famine is of your own making, even as mine was when Jamie and I first got married and I quit my job, God still loves you and can provide for you regardless of what you've done. I eventually learned that if you don't work, you don't eat (2 Thess. 3:10), but until then, God was merciful and faithful. He loved us and brought us through, despite my stupidity. He can do the same for you.

That's because God's dealings with us are according to our covenant, not our performance. Isaac was the heir of the covenant God made with Abraham, just like we are the heirs of the covenant the Lord made with Jesus. We are heirs and joint heirs with Him (Rom. 8:17). We get God's goodness because of faith and not because we deserve it.

That's not to say that our actions aren't important. Isaac obeyed the word from God and stayed in a land that was being devastated by famine. If he weren't in faith, he would have rejected what the Lord told him and taken the natural way out by going to Egypt, where there was no famine. He also wouldn't have planted seeds during a drought if he didn't believe that the Lord was going to make his crops grow. Isaac had faith, and it manifested itself through his actions.

Faith alone saves, but saving faith is never alone. As James said,

> *Even so faith, if it hath not works, is dead, being alone.*
>
> James 2:17

It's not our actions that save us. Faith is the victory that overcomes the world (1 John 5:4). We are saved by grace through faith (Eph. 2:8), but a true, biblical faith will always produce actions. Actions are just the fruit of true faith. So, Isaac did have to act, but as his actions with Rebekah proved, his actions weren't perfect. Ours aren't either. The Lord has never had anyone qualified working for Him yet. Don't let Satan disqualify you because you haven't done everything perfectly.

We must not become so introspective in hard times that we lose confidence in our God, who has promised us victory over all the power of the enemy. Regardless of what is going on in the world, our God will supply our needs according to His riches in glory by Christ Jesus (Phil. 4:19). He isn't bound by the financial limitations of this world. Just as the Lord blessed Jamie and me with that supply of fish, even though I wasn't working, so the Lord still loves you and will meet your needs if you will just trust Him.

In the beginning of our ministry, we used to struggle financially all the time. As I've already shared, most of it was because of my own stupidity. But in 1996, I got a revelation on financial prosperity that changed everything. We began to prosper as never before.

However, recently, we experienced a decrease in our income for the first time in nearly thirty years. Although we were only a couple of days late with our payments, we actually had creditors calling about when they would be paid. That really bothered me. I hate that, and I know the Lord does too.

I began to examine myself and question if this was a famine I had created. I had others tell me that I caused this problem by overwhelming our partners with the fact that our Charis campus buildout could cost as much as one billion dollars. They said it overwhelmed people and made them feel that their gift was insignificant.

We also announced Mike and Carrie Pickett as the ones to carry on our ministry after our promotion to glory. I went out of my way to make it clear that I was planning on a long life and am busier than ever, sharing the truths the Lord has given me. Yet, I had a couple of people ask me how I'm enjoying retirement. Nothing could be further from the truth.

I have gone from one thirty-minute TV program per day to having five daily programs, three of which are an hour long. This is in addition to regularly ministering at Charis Bible College and overseeing a ministry with 1100 employees. Yet I was told that some people thought the reason we announced our successors was because I had quit, and therefore, they quit their support.

All of this caused me to become introspective and wonder if I had caused the drought in our finances. That's when the Lord spoke to me through these very scriptures in Genesis 26. Isaac certainly didn't do everything right. He feared and was willing to let a man take his wife into his harem (Gen. 26:6-11); yet the Lord blessed Isaac with a hundred-fold return in one year.

> *Then Isaac sowed in that land, and received in the same year an hundredfold: and the LORD blessed him.*
>
> Genesis 26:12

That got my eyes off myself and any mistakes I'd made and put my attention back on the Word of God. If the Lord blessed Isaac in spite of his failings, I knew He would bless me through my faith in what Jesus did for me.

This quickened my faith, and in a short period of time, we regained our momentum and even got ahead financially. These same truths that worked for me and Isaac will work for you too.

23

## Get a Specific Word from God

Isaac's story also reveals that there isn't just one way of dealing with the potential famines that we find ourselves in. Abraham, Isaac's father, experienced a famine in the same land decades before Isaac's famine, but he dealt with it totally differently. Abraham went down into Egypt, where there was plenty of water, and escaped the famine that way (Gen. 12:10). That was an option.

But Isaac had the Lord appear to him and tell him to stay in the land during the famine.

> *And the LORD appeared unto him, and said, Go not down into Egypt; dwell in the land which I shall tell thee of:*
>
> Genesis 26:2

Isaac had a specific word from God. That's what makes all the difference. There is no substitute for a relationship with the Lord where we gain specific guidance for our personal situation. What worked in the past or for others may not necessarily work for us the same way. We need to hear directly from the Lord about what He wants us to do.

Look at the Israelites' conquest of the Promised Land; they had one of the greatest battle plans of all time in their fight against Jericho. The Lord had them just shout, and the massive walls fell down flat. Nothing like that had ever happened before. It was totally miraculous, but they never used that plan again. This was a specific plan for that one battle that Joshua received directly from the Lord (Josh. 5:13–6:5).

## What Is God's Word to You?

We have words from God too. The Lord has promised us that He will bless whatever we set our hand unto (Deut. 28:8). No weapon that is formed against us will prosper (Is. 54:17). He wishes above everything else that we prosper and be in health, even as our soul prospers (3 John 1:2). Jesus became poor so that we could become rich (2 Cor. 8:9).

The Lord has given us ample promises of His faithfulness to provide for us just like He gave to Isaac.

That's not the question. The real issue is, do we believe the Lord more than what our famine circumstances are telling us?

If we truly believe God's promises about prospering us at all times (2 Cor. 2:14 and 1 John 5:4), then we shouldn't panic during a famine. Hard times have come before, and people have survived and prospered. What God has done for others or us in the past, He will do again. Famines will come again, and those who trust in God will prosper as others have before them.

So, I would summarize the first step in reaping a hundredfold in a year of famine as, "Don't panic; put this into the perspective of history and recognize that God's promises still hold true, regardless of how bad the situation is. Next, you need to get a word from the Lord as Isaac did. We all have general words from the Lord about how He wants to meet our needs, which I've already listed. Those should give us faith (Rom. 10:17), but we need a specific word about our individual situation.

Genesis 26:2-6 says,

*And the LORD appeared unto him, and said, Go not down into Egypt; dwell in the land which I shall tell thee of: Sojourn in this land, and I will be with thee, and will bless thee; for unto thee, and unto thy seed, I will give all these countries, and I will perform the oath which I sware unto Abraham thy father; And I will make thy seed to multiply as the stars of heaven, and will give unto thy seed all these countries; and in thy seed shall all the nations of the earth be blessed; Because that Abraham obeyed my voice, and kept my charge, my commandments, my statutes, and my laws. And Isaac dwelt in Gerar:*

The Lord could have met Isaac's need in many ways, but He gave Isaac specific instructions to stay in the land of Gerar. If Isaac had gone somewhere else, he would have missed God's hundredfold provision. I have an entire teaching entitled, Y*our Place Called There*. It's part of my series based on 1 Kings 17:4, where the Lord told Elisha He had sent his provision **there**. The Lord didn't command the ravens to bring Elisha's food to where he was, but where God told him to go.

It's like a quarterback throwing a ball to his receiver. He doesn't throw the ball to where the receiver is, but where he is supposed to be. Likewise, many don't receive God's supply because they aren't all *there*. You can't wait for God's provision to come to you where you are, then obey His leading. You must do what the Lord has told you to do, and God's supply will come to you *there*, where He told you to go, and while you're doing what He told you to do.

This specific direction from the Lord only comes through your personal relationship with the Lord. I often have people ask me what they are supposed to do in hard times. I can give general directions from God's Word, but there is no substitute for hearing from the Lord directly about your individual situation. The Lord wants to speak to you more than you want to hear what He has to say. That's often the problem right there.

We have to separate ourselves from the distractions of this world and draw near to God (James 4:8) so we can hear His still small voice (1 Kgs. 19:12). He's always speaking, but His voice can be drowned out by the many voices of this life. As Psalm 46:10 says,

*"Be still, and know that I am God."*

Are you doing what the Lord has told you to do (your place called "there")? You can't prosper doing your own thing and asking God to bless it. There is a supernatural flow of God's anointing and provision when you are in the center of His will that doesn't function when you are anywhere else.

Are you like Isaac, acting on a specific word from the Lord, or are you just trying to cope like everyone else does in famine situations? One word from Jesus allowed Peter to walk on the water (Matt. 14:29). All the disciples could have done the same thing, but they were afraid to get out of the boat. That's strange when you consider the boat was full of water and going to sink. Why are we so afraid to break from the crowd and get out of the natural way of doing things when what everyone else is doing isn't working? We need to step out on God's Word and keep our eyes on Jesus, instead of the storm.

That's not to say there won't ever be problems when you are following the Lord. Paul said in 1 Corinthians 16:9,

*For a great door and effectual is opened unto me, and there are many adversaries.*

Paul was in the center of God's will in Ephesus, but there was a lot of opposition. However, God's supply was greater than the devil's attacks. Paul stayed in Ephesus for over three years and established a mighty work there that was a center of Christianity into the third century A.D.

The Lord spoke to me in 2008 during what people often refer to as "The Great Recession." The stock market took a huge hit, and investors were committing suicide because of the financial crisis. I believe it would be appropriate to call that a financial famine. But at the height of that crisis, the Lord told me it was time to begin the largest building project we had ever undertaken. We purchased 157 acres in Woodland Park, Colorado, and began making plans to build a campus for our Charis Bible College.

In the natural, this looked like the worst time to do something like that. There were over a hundred parachurch ministries in the Colorado Springs area that cut their budgets by 15-25%, anticipating a downturn in their receipts. But the Lord was leading me to increase our expenditures by millions of dollars. It turned out that we built over 100 million dollars' worth of buildings in nine and a half years, debt free. It was reaping one hundredfold in a *decade* of famine.

I had a word from God that went against all conventional wisdom, but it worked because it was *a word from God*. Any word from God is greater than anything the devil or the world can throw against it. You need a specific word from the Lord, like Isaac got, in order to reap a hundredfold in a year of famine.

How can you get a word from God or decide if what you are believing is truly a word from God or just your carnal thinking? I happen to have a great little booklet on that entitled *Four Basics of Hearing God's Voice*. Without going into all the details that I did in that booklet, let me say that the Lord's Word (the Bible) is the most basic and clear way to be led by the Lord. But He can and does give us very specific direction through the desires of our hearts.

Psalm 37:4 says,

> *Delight thyself also in the Lord; and he shall give thee the desires of thine heart.*

This isn't a promise that the Lord will give you anything you want. But it's a promise that when you are delighting in the Lord, the Lord will put His desires in your heart.

To illustrate this, I had a miraculous encounter with the Lord on March 23, 1968. My whole life was turned right side up. I fell in love with the Lord and have never gotten over it. One of the very first things that happened to me was that the Lord totally changed the desires of my heart. That was God's specific word to me.

Prior to that experience, I was on my own, attending my first year of college, and I was loving it. I was having the time of my life. But after that encounter, everything changed. I lost interest in everything but the Lord. I was consumed with just knowing Jesus in a deeper and more real way. I lost all desire to be in college, even though that made no sense. I was getting money from the government to attend college, and if I quit, I would lose it. I had a deferment from the draft as long as I stayed in school, and I had the acceptance of all my family and friends. It seemed like the craziest thing to contemplate dropping out of college, but that's what I suddenly wanted to do.

It actually went way beyond just wanting to quit college. I got to where I hated going to college. I don't have the words to convey how much it grieved me when, just a few days before, I loved it. There was a total about-face in my desires that was so drastic I couldn't ignore it.

So, I told everyone I was going to quit school. That caused no small stir. My mother didn't talk to me for two weeks, and when I finally took her out to eat, I said, "You've got to say something." She responded by saying, "I'm so ashamed." My mother and I had become best friends after my father died when I was twelve. My brother and sister were older and were pretty much gone, so it was just the two of us during my teenage years. It really affected me to think I had brought her to shame.

I was told by all but just a couple of people on this planet that I was crazy. They said the Lord wouldn't tell me not to get an education. Even if I wanted to go into the ministry, I needed to go to seminary. Plus, this was during the height of the Vietnam War. I was sure to be drafted if I dropped out of college.

This unexpected criticism stunned me. My mother pleaded with me to at least stay through the end of the semester so that if I came to my senses and wanted to go back, I wouldn't have my record tainted by dropping out.

So, I stayed, but it was torture for me. I can't tell you how much it grieved my heart. I actually had nightmares about it. My heart wasn't in it. My desires had totally changed.

Then one evening, I read Romans 14:23, which said,

...*whatsoever* is *not of faith is sin.*

That shook me to my core. I certainly wasn't in faith that I was supposed to stay in school. I was only doing it because of all the criticism that had come my way when I mentioned quitting. I realized that I had to make a decision, and I was determined to make it that night. I wasn't going to be in sin the next day.

But how could I tell if this was really the Lord or just my own desire to quit school?

I heard a sermon when I was a kid that said if you want to know what the Lord's will is, just do the opposite of what you want to do. In other words, don't follow the desires of your heart. That may be true for a carnal Christian who does not delight in the Lord and allow Him to shape the desires of their heart (Ps. 37:4). But I was more in love with the Lord than I had ever been. The Lord was truly the only delight of my heart. So, I began to lean towards thinking it was the Lord who had changed my desires.

The Lord also directed me towards Colossians 3:15, which says,

*And let the peace of God rule in your hearts…*

The Greek word *brabeuó*, which was translated "rule" in that verse, means "to arbitrate, i.e. (genitive case) to govern (figuratively, prevail)."[4] It comes from a root word meaning "umpire." I had to let the peace of God prevail, govern, rule, and act like an umpire in this decision-making process.

So, I thought of my options: stay in school or quit. Those were the only two options as far as I could see. I didn't feel total peace about either option. If I quit school, I was going to face a lot of rejection, loss of money, and possibly be killed in Vietnam. None of those things brought me peace. But when I contemplated staying in school, there was absolutely no peace whatsoever. In fact, I was certain I just couldn't do it.

Therefore, believing that I was delighting in the Lord with all my heart, and having lost all desire for college, I let the peace I felt about leaving school be the umpire in my life, and I decided to quit. I went to sleep in peace that night for the first time in several weeks.

In the morning, since I was still young in the Lord and unsure of my decision, I thought I would test it out. I went to the three people who had criticized me the most for even daring to think about quitting school, and I told them my decision. I was braced for their attack, but it didn't come. In fact, one of my worst critics got teary-eyed and said they would give anything to be in my shoes. I was shocked.

I asked why they felt that way, and they said they were in their fifties and had never known for certain that they were in the center of God's will. They were envious of me because the Lord had given me direction at such a young age.

By the end of that day, I had lost all doubt about what the Lord wanted me to do. I knew I was delighting in the Lord more than ever before. The Lord had spoken to me by changing the desires of my heart, and I had let the peace of God rule in my heart. I knew I had a word directly from the Lord. That decision turned out to be one of the best and most important of my life. It sustained me through Vietnam and put my life on a course that brought me to where I am today.

Even my mother came around to being my biggest supporter. She actually had a dream where the Lord told her I was doing exactly what He told me to do, and she should get behind me. She certainly did. She worked for me for twenty years, opening our mail and making deposits. She was a wonderful blessing in my life.

To summarize, the first thing you have to do is put everything into perspective. There have been famines before, and there will be famines again. This is nothing unusual, and the Lord is still faithful and has created the supply before you have the need. Cast your care on the Lord, knowing that He cares for you.

Then, you have to have a word from the Lord about what He wants you to do. You can't just copy what someone else has done to overcome their famine. What is the Lord saying to you? Make sure you are putting the Lord first in your life and then let the peace of God rule in your heart, regardless of how crazy it might seem to you or to others. You need a specific word from the Lord.

Next, notice that Isaac planted seed in a year of famine. They were in a drought. Others didn't plant because they thought it was a waste of time and seed. Without rain, the seed would die. But without planting seeds, you can't reap a harvest. Isaac took a risk and sowed in obedience to God's word, believing that the Lord would make it grow.

And grow it did. Isaac received a hundredfold return on his sowing in one year. And this was while others hadn't planted any seed because they thought it couldn't grow. So, Isaac had a corner on the market when his seed matured and sold for top dollar. This brought him more prosperity than anything he had ever done before.

Many had headed for Egypt to survive the famine, and those who remained were depleting all their resources to buy food at a premium. Yet, the person who got a word from the Lord and acted in faith was prospering as never before.

That's all it takes. We just need to hear from the Lord and then act.

Notice this: Isaac had a word from the Lord to stay in the land of Gerar, but the Lord didn't say anything to him about planting seed. He only had a word to stay put and not follow everyone else to Egypt to escape the famine. Isaac's planting of seed was not a specific instruction from the Lord, but a general law the Lord established at creation about seed, time, and harvest. Without planting seed, and giving it time, there can be no harvest.

So, Isaac had a word from the Lord, but then he did something practical too. There's a lesson in this for us.

The Lord is going to use people to supply our need. As Luke 6:38 says,

> *Give, and it shall be given unto you; good measure, pressed down, and shaken together, and running over, shall men give into your bosom. For with the same measure that ye mete withal it shall be measured to you again.*

Notice that this verse says the Lord will cause men to give into your bosom. As I said before, our monetary system is a man-made system. God didn't create it. He can use it, but the Lord doesn't give money to us directly. He gives us power or the ability to get wealth (Deut. 8:18), but He is not going to rain money down on you out of the sky. He blesses what we set our hand unto (Deut. 28:8). One hundred times zero is zero. We have to give the Lord something to work with.

Isaac planted seeds in the ground. That's what he set his hand unto. What have you set your hand unto? You can't just pray and wait on the Lord to do something. He's going to do something through people, and it's usually the very people that you have sown something into that the Lord uses to give back to you.

Every one of us has something we can sow. It might be a product that you sell, or it could be your work and talents God has given you. With me, I have a calling to minister God's Word, and as I give what He has given me, I reap it back in finances (1 Cor. 9:14). I sow God's Word into people's lives, and I reap back finances (Gal. 6:6-7).

During the recent financial problem I mentioned, I told my partners that we needed extra support to meet our basic needs. One of the ministries I donate to monthly texted me, saying they were sending a financial gift to help us, and they mentioned that if we needed to reduce or eliminate our giving to them, they would understand. I immediately texted them back and told them that my giving would be the very last thing I would ever decrease.

Giving or sowing is an absolute necessity in reaping a harvest. I will never quit sowing regardless of how severe my financial crisis might be. **The worst thing you can do in a famine is decrease your giving.**

When I'm in financial need, I increase my giving. You can't reap if you don't sow, and the more you sow, the more you will reap (2 Cor. 9:6). During this same financial crunch, I sent out one of my new books to sixty thousand people, free of charge. I was sowing seeds for a harvest.

Sowing financial seeds and waiting for a harvest is putting natural laws into motion. Isaac had a supernatural word from the Lord about how the Lord would prosper him if he stayed in a land that was experiencing a drought. But Isaac didn't just sit on that word and do nothing. He planted seeds.

**You can't reap a hundredfold if you don't plant seeds.**

I remember reading a summary by George Barna about a survey he took during "The Great Recession." He said the number one way that Christians dealt with their financial decrease was to cut back on their giving. That shocked me! That's the last thing that should ever happen. I do just the opposite.

In a time of famine, people tend to look at the seeds they have and desire to eat them instead of planting some of them. I understand that. Hunger can get us into short-term thinking, but the result of that is even greater hunger down the road. We have to discipline ourselves to think long term. We can't eat all the seeds in our hands. By faith, we have to plant some of them in hope of a harvest. Don't mortgage your future for the present. That is a sure-fire way to guarantee even greater hunger in the future.

So, Isaac stayed in a situation that looked impossible because he had a word from the Lord. But he also operated in faith and did what he needed to do in the natural, regardless of the naysayers who thought it was useless. This caused him to prosper so much that the unbelievers envied him and said he was greater than them.

> *And the man waxed great, and went forward, and grew until he became very great: For he had possession of flocks, and possession of herds, and great store of servants: and the Philistines envied him.*
>
> Genesis 26:13-14

Notice the use of the word "waxed." This describes Isaac becoming prosperous over time. It's drawing an illustration from the way candles were made, where a wick was repeatedly dipped in hot wax, each dip putting a thin layer of wax over the wick. This had to be repeated hundreds of times until the entire candle was formed. Likewise, God's prosperity is not a one-time, get-rich-quick scheme. It is doing what the Lord tells you to do over a long period of time. And look at the result that was produced in Isaac's life.

*And Abimelech said unto Isaac, Go from us; for thou art much mightier than we.*

Genesis 26:16

When was the last time a leader of a city told you to leave because you were greater than them? I've actually had that happen to me. Of course, Woodland Park, Colorado, where I live, is a small city of 7,500, but they threatened to de-annex our ministry from the city because our resources are much greater than the whole city. There are some in the city government who ignore all the benefit we bring to them and only focus on what they provide for us.

After Abimelech had cast Isaac out of Gerar, he came back to Isaac and wanted to make a covenant with him. Isaac was shocked and asked why he wanted to covenant with him since he had driven him away. Abimelech said it was because he finally realized that Isaac was "*the blessed of the LORD*," so he wanted peace between them (Gen. 26:26-30). I claim that for myself. Someday, the leaders of my city will recognize that they are blessed to have our employees and students living, working, and spending money in this city. They will come around to recognizing we are the blessed of the Lord and will want to make a covenant with us.

And here's another great thing that happened the same day Isaac made that covenant with Abimelech. His servants found water in a well. Water is a major issue in Colorado. Water in Colorado is actually more expensive than gold, and water rights have been a source of contention between the city and us. I believe that at the same time they come around to making peace with us, the water rights will be resolved too. Amen!

So, Isaac had a supernatural word from the Lord that gave him direction, but he also did what was prudent in the natural in order to reap this hundredfold return. When we do what we can in the natural, God puts His super on it, and the results are supernatural.

It's like the time Peter was asked if Jesus paid taxes (Matt. 17:24). Jesus told him to go to the sea and cast in a hook and inside the mouth of the first fish he caught would be a coin to pay their taxes (Matt. 17:27). That was a supernatural word of knowledge from the Lord. It was absolutely miraculous that the Lord had a fish swallow the exact coin needed and that Peter could just cast a hook into the sea and catch that exact fish. Wow!

But the Lord didn't just rain the money down from heaven. The Lord didn't create that money in the fish's mouth. That would be counterfeiting. Money is a man-made system. The Lord knew that someone had lost that money in the sea. The Lord knew the fish had swallowed that coin, and He had Peter do something as simple as go fishing. Peter cast a hook into the water, and Jesus had that fish bite the hook. There was a combination of the natural and the supernatural for Peter to receive that supply.

## Conclusion

Famines come and go. Whatever problem you are facing today, others have faced similar things before and come through. You can too.

There isn't just one way of dealing with the famines that come against you. You need a specific word from the Lord about what He wants you to do in your situation. Once you receive that direction, act on it, regardless of what conventional wisdom says.

Also, recognize that there will be things you need to do in the natural too. The Lord doesn't just rain money down from heaven. As Deuteronomy 8:18 says, the Lord gives you power to get wealth. You have to use that power in faith to see the tangible money come into being.

And one of the absolutely indispensable things we need to do is to sow seed. You can't have a harvest if you haven't sown any seed.

I pray this brief study about how Isaac reaped a hundredfold in a year of famine helped you as much as it has helped me. Although I had seen these truths before, the Lord spoke them to me anew during the financial famine I recently experienced. He also told me this was too good to keep to myself. I needed to share this with others so they could benefit from it too.

As you put these truths into practice in your life, get ready for a hundredfold increase. The supply is already on the way.

## FURTHER STUDY

If you enjoyed this booklet and would like to learn more about some of the things I've shared, I suggest my teachings:

- *Four Basics of Hearing God's Voice*
- *Lessons from Elijah (Your Place Called There)*
- *Financial Stewardship*

Plus 200,000 hours of free teaching on our website.

These teachings are available for free at **awmi.net** or can be purchased at **awmi.net/store**.

Go deeper in your relationship with God by browsing all of Andrew's free teachings.

# Receive Jesus as Your Savior

Choosing to receive Jesus Christ as your Lord and Savior is the most important decision you'll ever make!

God's Word promises, *"That if thou shalt confess with thy mouth the Lord Jesus, and shalt believe in thine heart that God hath raised him from the dead, thou shalt be saved. For with the heart man believeth unto righteousness; and with the mouth confession is made unto salvation"* (Rom. 10:9–10). *"For whosoever shall call upon the name of the Lord shall be saved"* (Rom. 10:13). By His grace, God has already done everything to provide salvation. Your part is simply to believe and receive.

Pray out loud: "Jesus, I acknowledge that I've sinned and need to receive what you did for the forgiveness of my sins. I confess that You are my Lord and Savior. I believe in my heart that God raised You from the dead. By faith in Your Word, I receive salvation now. Thank You for saving me."

The very moment you commit your life to Jesus Christ, the truth of His Word instantly comes to pass in your spirit. Now that you're born again, there's a brand-new you!

Please contact us and let us know that you've prayed to receive Jesus as your Savior. We'd like to send you some free materials to help you on your new journey. Call our Helpline: **719-635-1111** (available 24 hours a day, seven days a week) to speak to a staff member who is here to help you understand and grow in your new relationship with the Lord.

Welcome to your new life!

# Receive the Holy Spirit

As His child, your loving heavenly Father wants to give you the supernatural power you need to live a new life. *"For every one that asketh receiveth; and he that seeketh findeth; and to him that knocketh it shall be opened... how much more shall* your *heavenly Father give the Holy Spirit to them that ask him?"* (Luke 11:10–13).

All you have to do is ask, believe, and receive! Pray this: "Father, I recognize my need for Your power to live a new life. Please fill me with Your Holy Spirit. By faith, I receive it right now. Thank You for baptizing me. Holy Spirit, You are welcome in my life."

Some syllables from a language you don't recognize will rise up from your heart to your mouth (1 Cor. 14:14). As you speak them out loud by faith, you're releasing God's power from within and building yourself up in the spirit (1 Cor. 14:4). You can do this whenever and wherever you like.

It doesn't really matter whether you felt anything or not when you prayed to receive the Lord and His Spirit. If you believed in your heart that you received, then God's Word promises you did. *"Therefore I say unto you, What things soever ye desire, when ye pray, believe that ye receive them, and ye shall have them"* (Mark 11:24). God always honors His Word—believe it!

We would like to rejoice with you, pray with you, and answer any questions to help you understand more fully what has taken place in your life!

Please contact us to let us know that you've prayed to be filled with the Holy Spirit and to request the book *The New You & the Holy Spirit*. This book will explain in more detail about the benefits of being filled with the Holy Spirit and speaking in tongues. Call our Helpline: **719-635-1111** (available 24 hours a day, seven days a week).

# Notes

1. *Merriam-Webster Dictionary*, s.v. "famine," accessed August 11, 2025, https://www.merriam-webster.com/dictionary/famine

2. *Strong's Definitions*, s.v. "râ'âb" ("בָּעֵר"), accessed August 11, 2025, https://www.blueletterbible.org/lexicon/h7458/kjv/wlc/0-1/

3. *Strong's Definitions*, s.v. "próskairos" ("πρόσκαιρος"), accessed August 11, 2025, https://www.blueletterbible.org/lexicon/g4340/kjv/tr/0-1/

4. *Strong's Definitions*, s.v. "brabeúō" ("βραβεύω"), accessed August 14, 2025, https://www.blueletterbible.org/lexicon/g1018/kjv/tr/0-1/

# Call for Prayer

If you need prayer for any reason, you can call our Helpline, 24 hours a day, seven days a week at **719-635-1111**. A trained prayer minister will answer your call and pray with you.

Every day, we receive testimonies of healings and other miracles from our Helpline, and we are ministering God's nearly-too-good-to-be-true message of the Gospel to more people than ever. So, I encourage you to call today!

# About the Author

Andrew Wommack's life was forever changed the moment he encountered the supernatural love of God on March 23, 1968. As a renowned Bible teacher and author, Andrew has made it his mission to change the way the world sees God.

Andrew's vision is to go as far and deep with the Gospel as possible. His message goes far through the *Gospel Truth* television program, which is available to over half the world's population. The message goes deep through discipleship at Charis Bible College, headquartered in Woodland Park, Colorado. Founded in 1994, Charis has campuses across the United States and around the globe.

Andrew also has an extensive library of teaching materials in print, audio, and video. More than 200,000 hours of free teachings can be accessed at **awmi.net**.

# Contact Information

Andrew Wommack Ministries, Inc.
PO Box 3333
Colorado Springs, CO 80934-3333
info@awmi.net
**awmi.net**

Helpline: 719-635-1111 (available 24/7)

**Charis Bible College**
info@charisbiblecollege.org
844-360-9577
**CharisBibleCollege.org**

For a complete list of all of our offices,
visit **awmi.net/contact-us**.

Connect with us on social media.

# Andrew Wommack's LIVING COMMENTARY DIGITAL STUDY BIBLE

Andrew Wommack's *Living Commentary* digital study Bible is a user-friendly, downloadable program. It's like reading the Bible with Andrew at your side, sharing his revelation with you verse by verse.

Main features:
- Bible study software with a grace-and-faith perspective
- Over 27,000 notes by Andrew on verses from Genesis through Revelation
- *Adam Clarke's Commentary on the Bible*
- *Albert Barnes' Notes on the Whole Bible*
- *Matthew Henry's Concise Commentary*
- 12 Bible versions
- 3 optional premium translation add-ons: *New Living Translation*, *New International Version*, and *The Message* (additional purchase of $9.99 each)
- 2 concordances: *Englishman's Concordance* and *Strong's Concordance*
- 2 dictionaries: *Collaborative International Dictionary* and *Holman's Dictionary*
- Atlas with biblical maps
- Bible and *Living Commentary* statistics
- Quick navigation, including history of verses
- Robust search capabilities (for the Bible and Andrew's notes)
- "Living" (i.e., constantly updated and expanding)
- Ability to create personal notes
- Accessible online and offline

Whether you're new to studying the Bible or a seasoned Bible scholar, you'll gain a deeper revelation of the Word from a grace-and-faith perspective.

Purchase Andrew's *Living Commentary* today at **awmi.net/living** and grow in the Word with Andrew.

Item code: 8350

ANDREW WOMMACK MINISTRIES

Get free streaming access to Andrew Wommack's library of faith building programs.

# GOSPEL TRUTH
### NETWORK

## GTNTV.com

Download our apps available on mobile and TV platforms or stream GTN on Comcast Xfinity.